Autism & PDD ™

Concept Development

Animals

Pam Britton Reese
Nena C. Challenner

Skill Areas:	Concept Development, Language
Ages:	3 through 8
Grades:	Preschool through 3rd

LinguiSystems, Inc.
3100 4th Avenue
East Moline, IL 61244-9700
1-800-PRO IDEA
1-800-776-4332

FAX: 1-800-577-4555
E-mail: service@linguisystems.com
Web: www.linguisystems.com
TDD: 1-800-933-8331
           (for those with hearing impairments)

Printed in the U.S.A.

ISBN 0-7606-0387-1

About the Authors

Pam Britton Reese, M.A., CCC-SLP, owns a private practice, CommunicAid Plus, where she provides speech and language services to children and adults. She is also an educational consultant to public and private schools. Pam has over nine years experience in the schools as a speech-language pathologist and teacher of the hearing-impaired. She has worked with children with autism and PDD since 1995. *Autism & PDD: Concept Development* is her fourth publication with LinguiSystems.

Nena C. Challenner, M.Ed., is a Community-Based Instruction Teacher and Inclusion Specialist. She has been a teacher for over 15 years and has taught preschool through second grade. She has worked with children with autism and PDD since 1995. Nena is also a reading consultant at CommunicAid Plus. *Autism & PDD: Concept Development* is her third publication with LinguiSystems.

Dedication

For the children at CommunicAid Plus (CAP Kids!)

Edited by Lauri Whiskeyman
Illustrations by Margaret Warner
Page Layout by Christine Buysse

Table of Contents

Introduction

In our work with children with autism, we were often surprised at misconceptions our students had about the world. For example, when 9-year-old Katie was asked, "What would you do if you saw a house on fire?" she answered, "Roast marshmallows." She had only experienced fire in this way and was unable to perceive that fire might also be dangerous, that it burns, or that it can heat a home. Other children with autism whom we have known didn't recognize a sitting dog as a dog or a rocking chair as a chair. These are concepts that typically-developing children are able to process through observing or listening to information and instantly linking to other learned concepts. We know that children with autism must be taught such language skills as naming attributes, placing words in appropriate categories, and giving descriptions.

It is well documented that children with autism learn more easily when information is presented in a visual format. The picture is constant and the child can view it until the concept is learned, as opposed to the transient nature of speech. Most books published for young children, however, do not teach the concepts the child with autism needs to learn. Although the stories are often engaging and the artwork of museum quality, they too often confuse the child with autism. Foxes that drive? Animals that wear clothing and talk? Cars with eyes? Although amusing, they are not a realistic depiction of our world. Often, too, the art is very complex with many extraneous details. (A list of some books we found that did a good job of teaching concepts is included on page 132.)

Each book in *Autism & PDD: Concept Development* covers 10 concepts around a theme:

- Animals
- Clothing
- Food
- Household Items
- Toys and Entertainment
- Transportation

Specific attributes and features of each concept are illustrated with large pictures, simple sentences, and picture symbols. In addition, there are questions to check comprehension and activities to help the child apply this knowledge to other contexts. These books were developed for professionals who work with children with autism, ages 3 through 8. However, these books can also be used with children who have language delays or language disorders caused by disabilities such as Down syndrome. Parents and caregivers can also use these stories and activities.

How to Use this Book

This book contains concepts about 10 different animals. Each concept is illustrated in both a large-page and mini-page format for making books to read to the child. We suggest that the large-page format be copied. Place the pages in plastic page protectors. Sliding a thin piece of cardboard or card stock into the pocket between the pages will stiffen the pages and make them easier for young children to turn. Put the pages into folders with brads or three-ring notebooks to create a book. You may want to put a copy of the first page of each unit on the front of the folder or notebook. The mini-pages can be made into small books for the children to take home after they've heard the story at school.

You may want to use all of the concepts in the book at one time to introduce or extend a thematic unit or you can select a specific concept to focus on. For example, a child might know dog and cat, but have no idea what a rabbit is! Remember to go at the child's pace. A child might need many lessons on chairs, for example, before moving on to other concepts in the book.

Comprehension Questions

A variety of comprehension questions (e.g., *yes-no, wh-, how*) follow each concept. The questions can be used in different ways. Some children may only be able to answer the *yes-no* questions. Some children may do better with the *wh-* and *how* questions. You can ask the questions after each concept is taught or after each page. If a child has difficulty answering a question, go through the targeted concept again and help him or her find the answer. Cue the child by pointing to the picture and/or text as you ask the question again.

Generalization Pages

Each concept has a generalization exercise. This exercise is designed to check the child's comprehension of the concept as well as to extend understanding of the concept to different forms and views. Many of the children we work with understand only one form of a concept: "That is a cat. That cat is gray. Thus, all cats must be gray or they are not cats." As you can see, that is a false generalization. By presenting variations of the same concept such as size, color, and position, the child learns to expand his or her mental definition of the concept.

After you read about the targeted concept, make a copy of the generalization page for the child. Read the directions aloud and have the child complete the page. Then encourage the child to describe the circled concepts. Depending on the child's level, the responses could be as simple as labeling "shirt" or as elaborate as "The shirt has long sleeves." You can also use the pictures on this page to point out the differences between the circled concepts.

Extension Activity

This activity is designed to extend instruction for any of the concepts in the book. Directions are found on the activity pages.

Introduction, *continued*

Suggested Literature

We have included a list of children's literature to help extend and promote generalization of the concepts to other contexts. These books were carefully chosen because of their simple text and realistic pictures. It is important to provide as many opportunities as possible for the child with autism to see and hear the concept. We have found that repeated exposure to the concepts in *Autism & PDD: Concept Development*, followed by other books with different pictures and texts, aids the child with autism in generalizing the concept to different contexts.

Closing

Remember that the concepts covered in the book can be taught in classrooms as well as group or individual therapy sessions. We hope that the children you work with enjoy the books as much as our students and clients do.

Pam and Nena

Dog

A dog is an animal.

A dog has four legs and a tail.

A dog has fur.

Some dogs are big. Some dogs are little.

A dog barks.

A dog is a pet.

puppy

A baby dog is called a puppy.

Dogs like to chew bones.

Concept: Dog

Yes-No Questions

1. Is a dog an animal?

2. Does a dog have three legs?

3. Does a dog have a tail?

4. Is a dog a pet?

5. Does a dog have feathers?

6. Are all dogs little?

7. Are some dogs little?

8. Do dogs meow?

9. Is a baby dog a calf?

10. Do dogs like to chew bones?

Wh- and How Questions

1. How many legs does a dog have?

2. What sound does a dog make?

3. What is a baby dog called?

4. What do dogs like to chew?

5. What has fur and a tail?

6. What is a dog: clothing or an animal?

7. What covers a dog's body?

8. What is a good pet?

9. What pet do you have?

10. Which do you like better: big dogs or little dogs?

Dog Generalization Page

Circle the dogs. Put an X on each picture that is not a dog.

Dog Mini-Book

Copy this page. Cut apart the boxes on the dotted lines. Put the story in order to make a little book and staple.

Dog

Autism & PDD: Concept Development

Cat

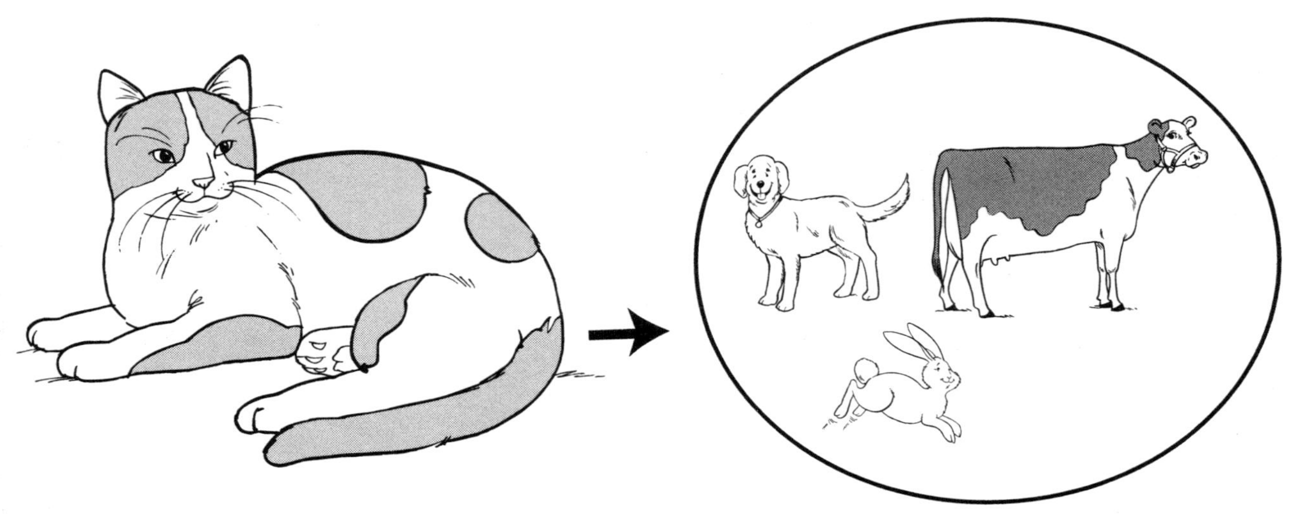

A cat is an animal.

 4  

A cat has four legs and a tail.

A cat has fur.

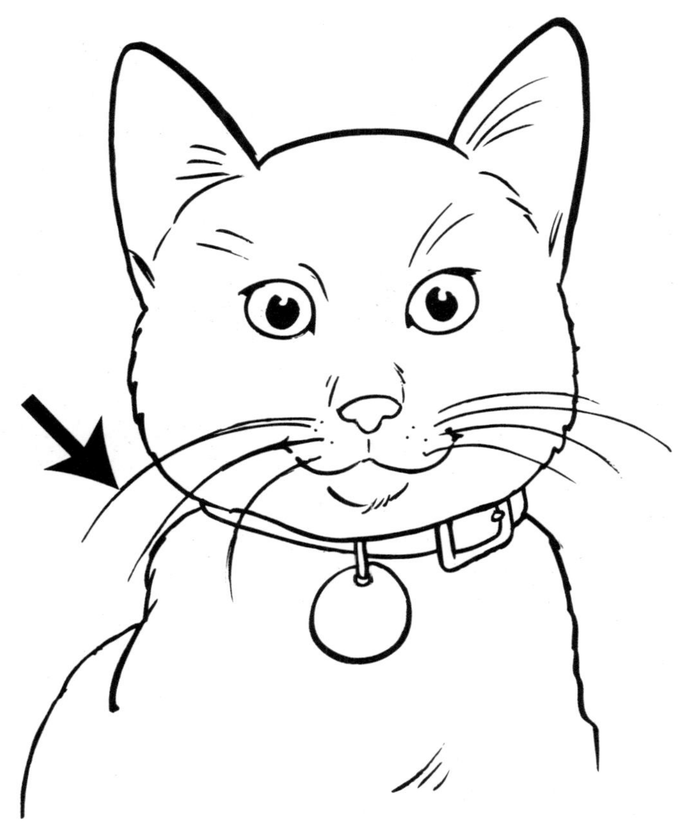

A cat has whiskers.

A cat can meow and purr.

kitten

A baby cat is called a kitten.

A cat is a pet.

Cats like to climb trees.

Concept: Cat

Yes-No Questions

1. Is a cat an animal?

2. Does a cat have four legs?

3. Does a cat have scales?

4. Does a cat have whiskers?

5. Can a cat bark?

6. Is a baby cat called a puppy?

7. Is a baby cat called a kitten?

8. Does a cat have a tail?

9. Do cats like to swim?

10. Do you have a cat?

Wh- and How Questions

1. How many legs does a cat have?

2. What are whiskers?

3. Where are the whiskers on a cat?

4. What sound can a cat make?

5. What is a baby cat called?

6. What covers a cat's body?

7. What do cats like to climb?

8. What is a cat: a toy or an animal?

9. Which pet can say, "Meow"?

10. When is a cat called a kitten?

Cat Generalization Page

Circle the cats. Put an X on each picture that is not a cat.

Cat Mini-Book

Copy this page. Cut apart the boxes on the dotted lines. Put the story in order to make a little book and staple.

Cat

Autism & PDD: Concept Development

Bird

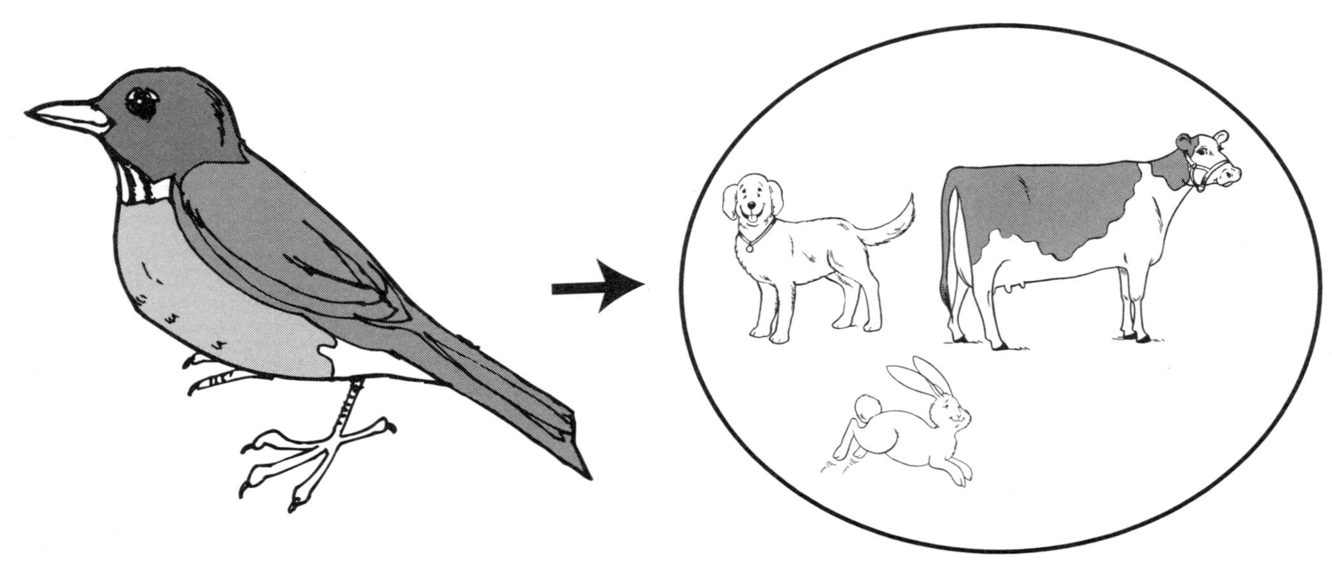

A bird is an animal.

A bird has wings.

A bird has feathers.

2

A bird has two legs and a beak.

A bird can fly.

A bird lives in a nest.

A bird can lay eggs.

A bird likes to eat worms.

Concept: Bird

Yes-No Questions

1. Is a bird a toy?

2. Is a bird an animal?

3. Does a bird have wings?

4. Does a bird have fur?

5. Does a bird have four legs?

6. Does a bird have a beak?

7. Can a bird fly?

8. Does a bird live in the water?

9. Can a bird lay eggs?

10. Do birds like to eat candy?

Wh- and How Questions

1. What animal has wings?

2. What covers a bird's body?

3. How many legs does a bird have?

4. What is a bird's mouth called?

5. Where do birds live?

6. What do birds lay in a nest?

7. What do birds like to eat?

8. What animal lays eggs?

9. What can fly in the sky?

10. What animal has a beak?

Bird Generalization Page

Circle the birds. Put an X on each picture that is not a bird.

Bird Mini-Book

Copy this page. Cut apart the boxes on the dotted lines. Put the story in order to make a little book and staple.

Bird

Autism & PDD: Concept Development

Fish

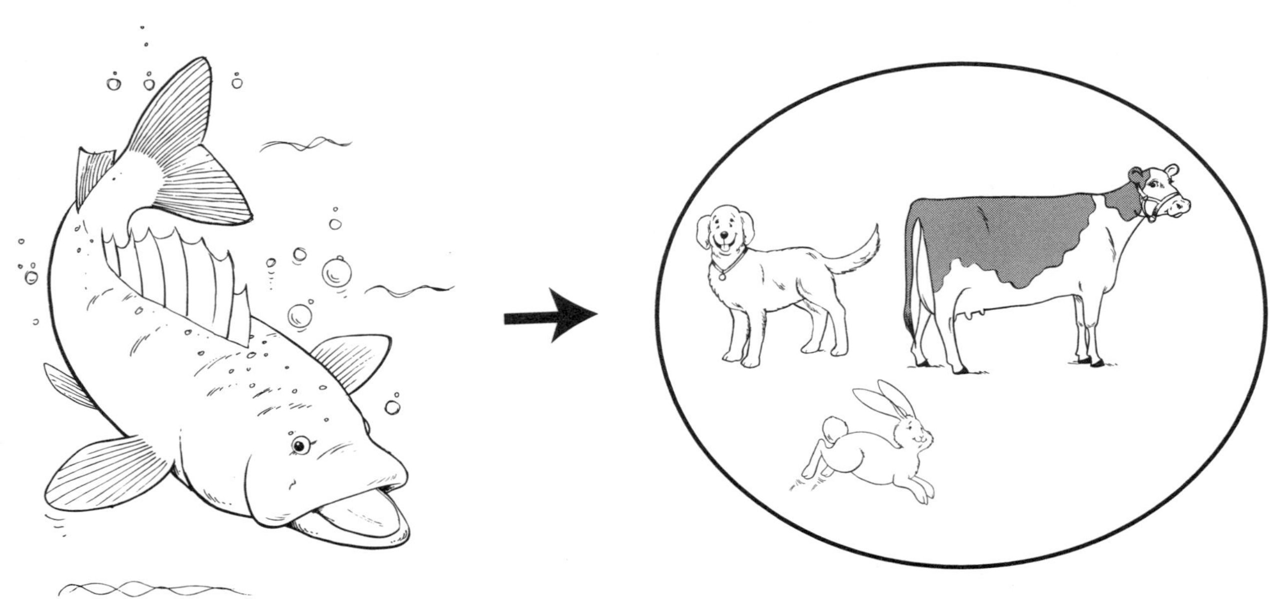

A fish is an animal.

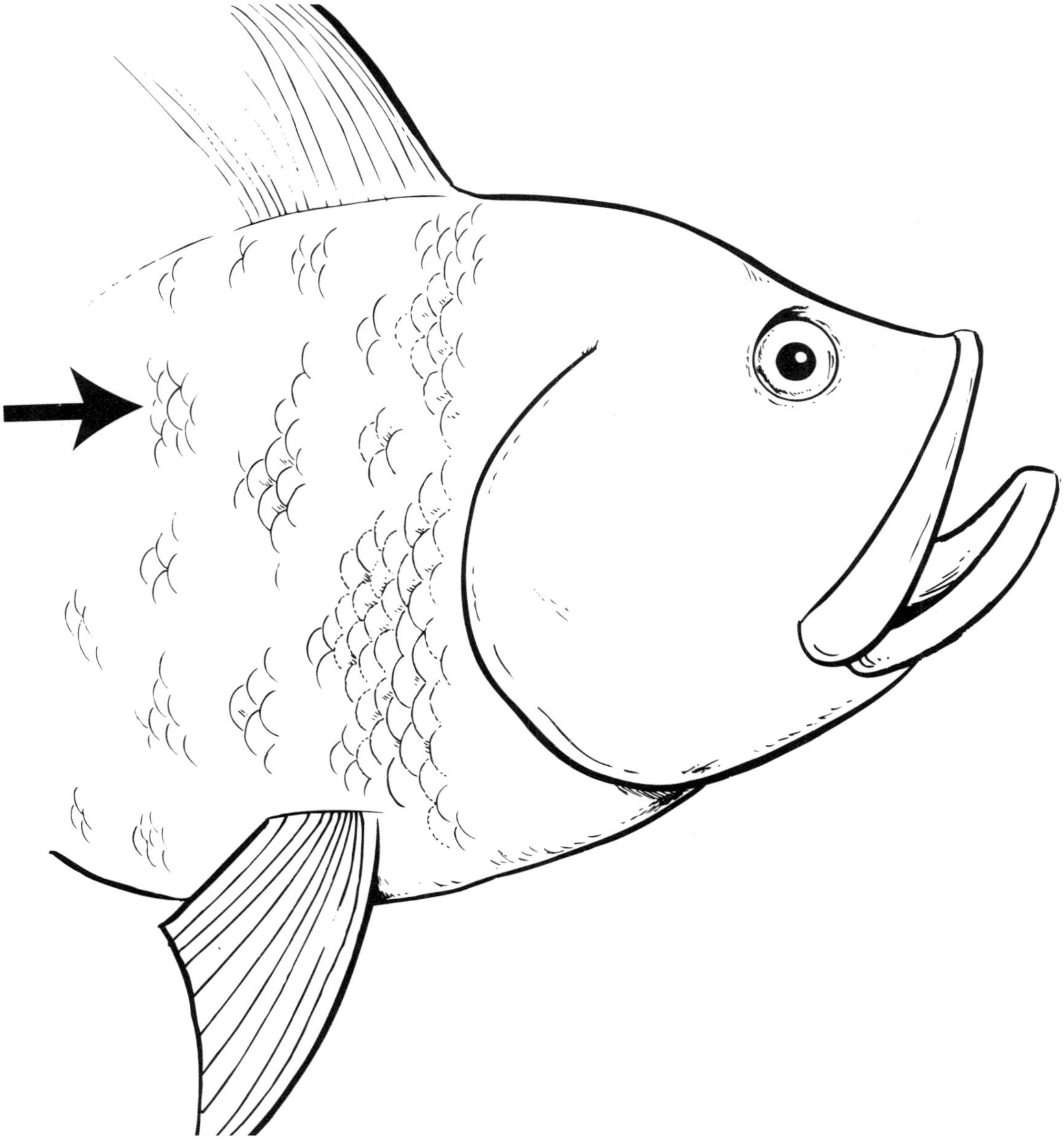

 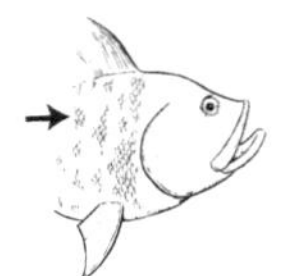

A fish has scales.

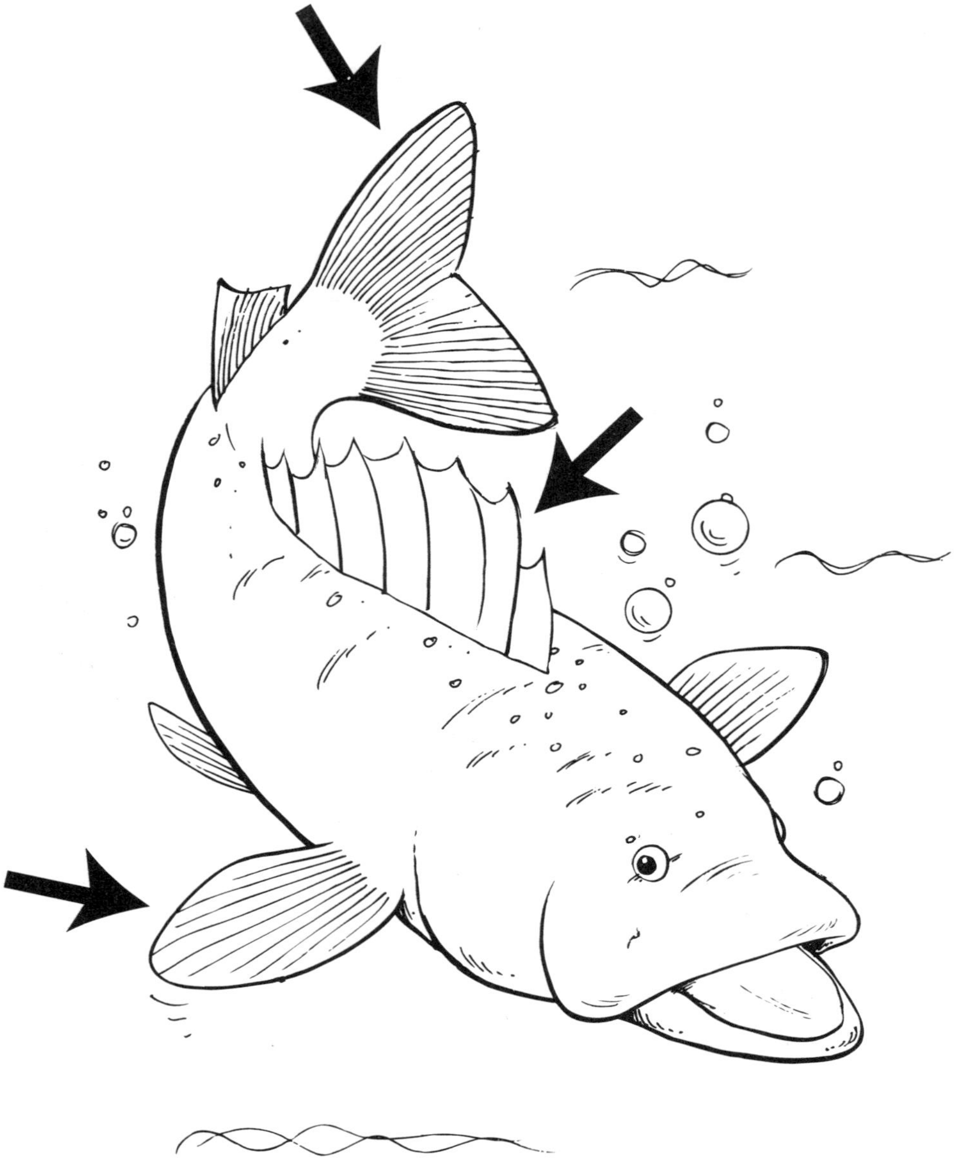

 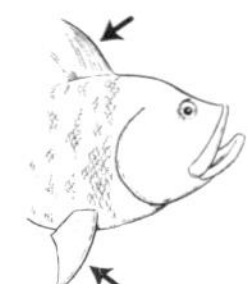 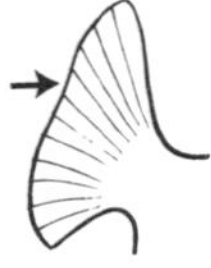

A fish has fins and a tail.

A fish lives in water.

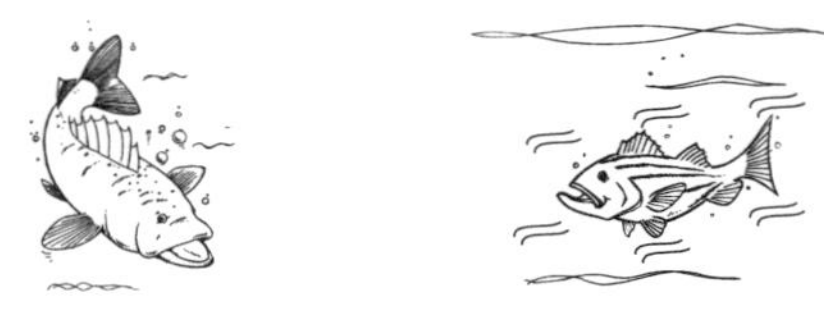

A fish swims.

Sometimes fish are pets.

Sometimes people catch fish.

Sometimes people eat fish.

Concept: Fish

Yes-No Questions

1. Is a fish an animal?
2. Does a fish have feathers?
3. Does a fish have scales?
4. Can a fish swim?
5. Does a fish live in a nest?
6. Does a fish have legs?
7. Can people catch fish?
8. Can a fish fly?
9. Does a fish have fins and a tail?
10. Do you have a fish?

Wh- and How Questions

1. What is a fish: a toy or an animal?
2. What animal has fins and a tail?
3. What covers a fish's body?
4. Where does a fish live?
5. How does a fish move?
6. Where do fish swim?
7. What do people do with fish?
8. Who eats fish?
9. Why do people catch fish?
10. Where is the tail on a fish?

Fish Generalization Page

Circle the fish. Put an X on each picture that is not a fish.

Fish Mini-Book

Copy this page. Cut apart the boxes on the dotted lines. Put the story in order to make a little book and staple.

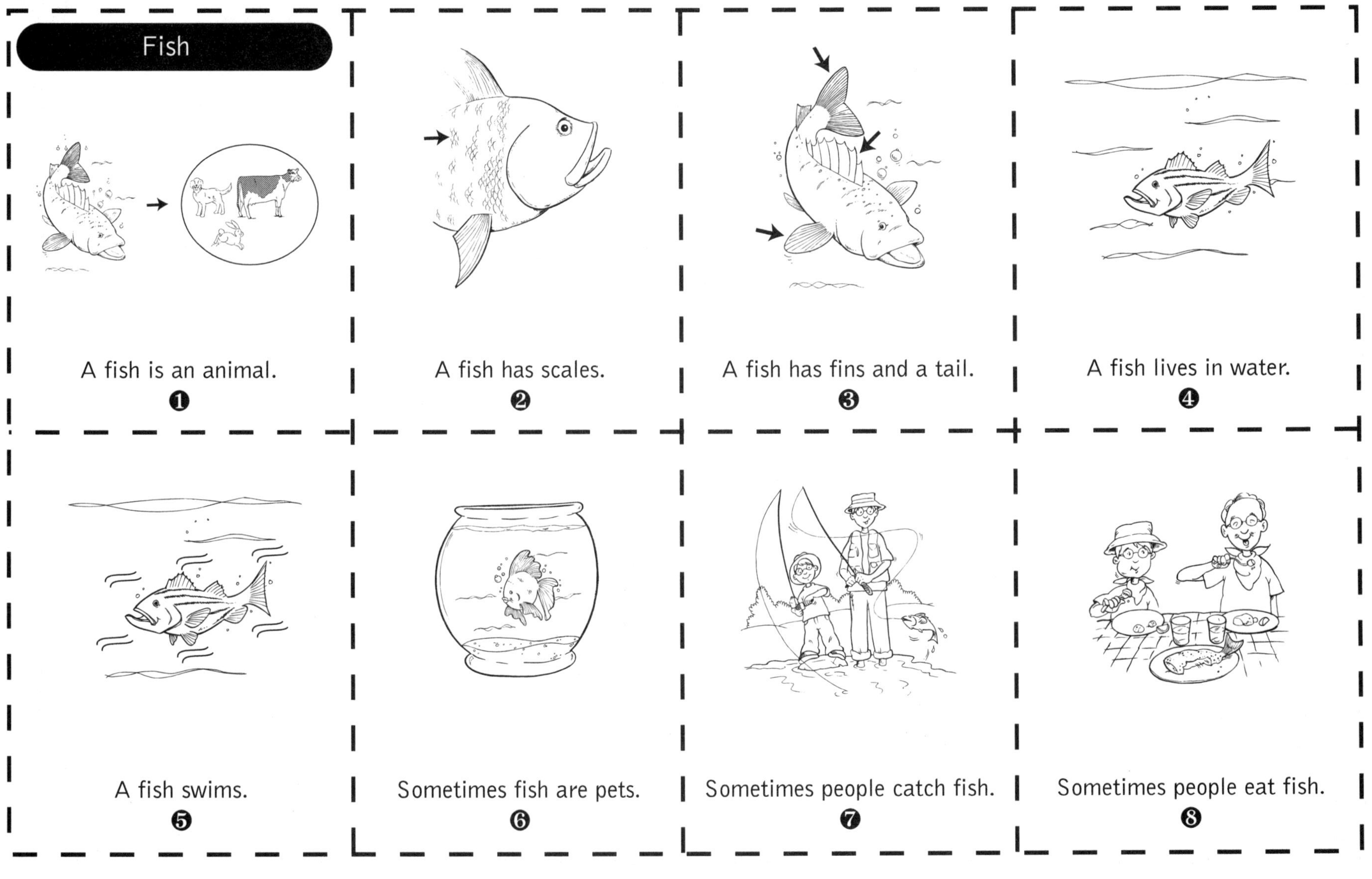

Fish

Autism & PDD: Concept Development

Rabbit

A rabbit is an animal.

Sometimes a rabbit is a pet.

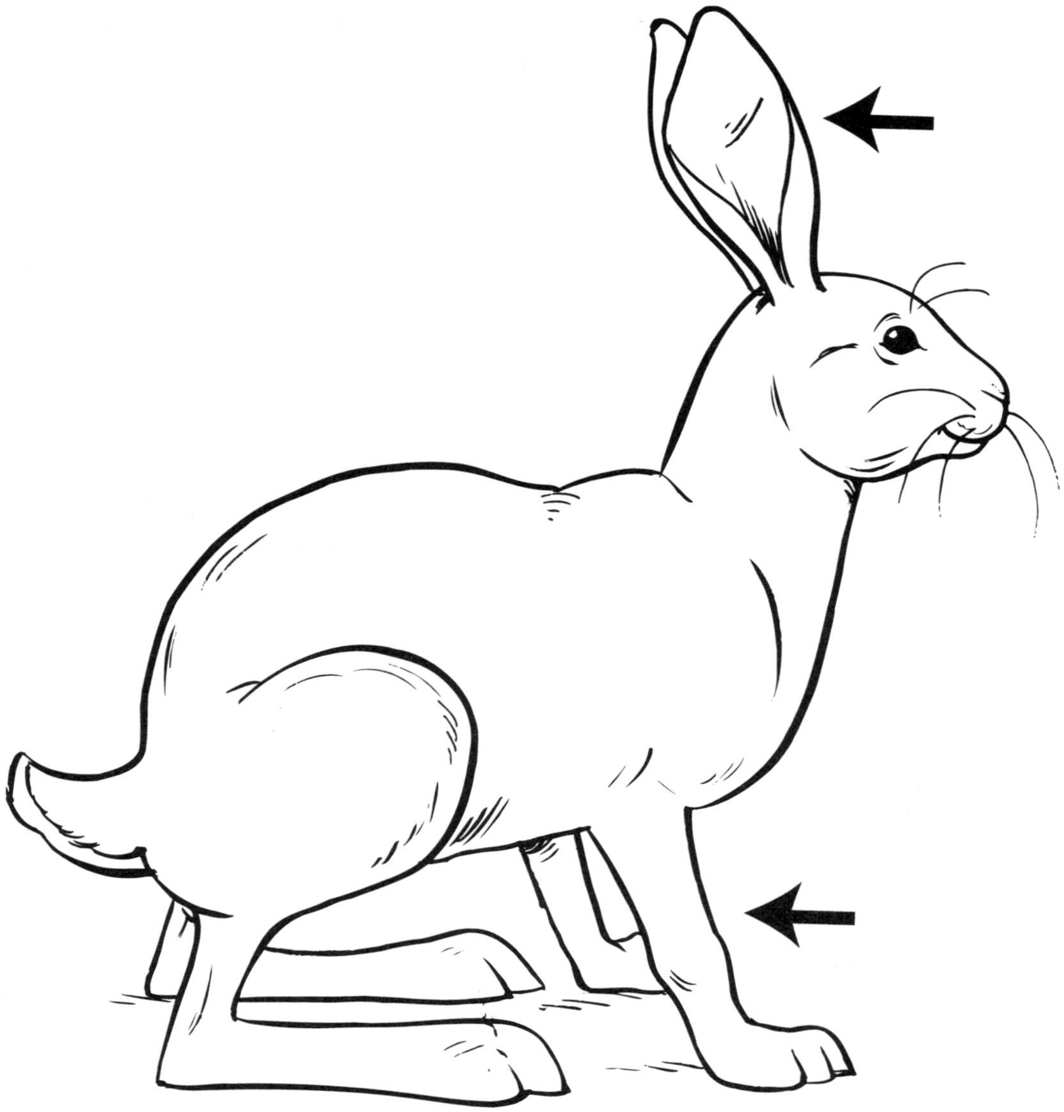

 2 ——  4 

A rabbit has two long ears and four legs.

A rabbit has a fluffy tail.

A rabbit has soft fur.

A rabbit hops.

A rabbit eats carrots.

bunny

Sometimes a rabbit is called a bunny.

Concept: Rabbit

Yes-No Questions

1. Is a rabbit an animal?

2. Can a rabbit be a pet?

3. Does a rabbit have two legs?

4. Does a rabbit have a tail?

5. Does a rabbit have feathers?

6. Does a rabbit swim?

7. Does a rabbit hop?

8. Does a rabbit eat chips?

9. Can a rabbit be called a bunny?

10. Is a rabbit a dog?

Wh- and How Questions

1. What is a rabbit: a toy or an animal?

2. How many ears does a rabbit have?

3. How many legs does a rabbit have?

4. What covers a rabbit's body?

5. How does a rabbit move?

6. What does a rabbit eat?

7. What is another name for a rabbit?

8. What kind of tail does a rabbit have?

9. What is a good pet?

10. How does a rabbit's fur feel?

Rabbit Generalization Page

Circle the rabbits. Put an X on each picture that is not a rabbit.

Rabbit Mini-Book

Copy this page. Cut apart the boxes on the dotted lines. Put the story in order to make a little book and staple.

Rabbit
Autism & PDD: Concept Development

Bee

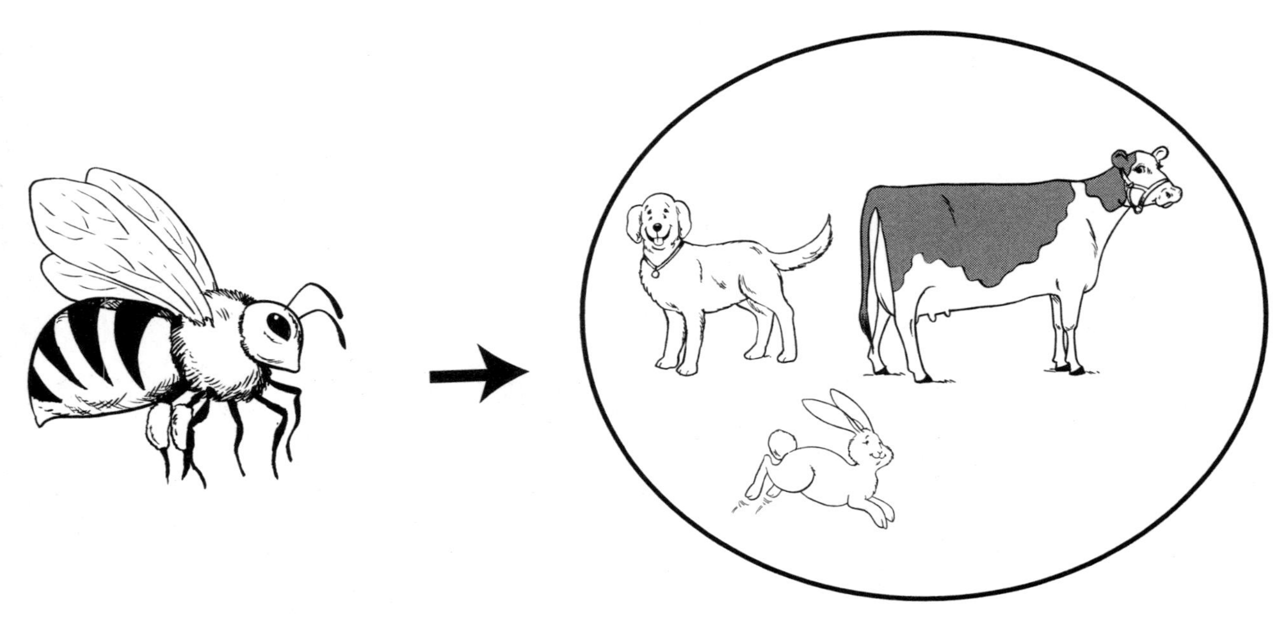

A bee is an animal.

  6 

A bee has wings and six legs.

A bee has black and yellow stripes.

A bee makes a "Bzzz" sound.

Sometimes a bee can sting.

A bee can fly.

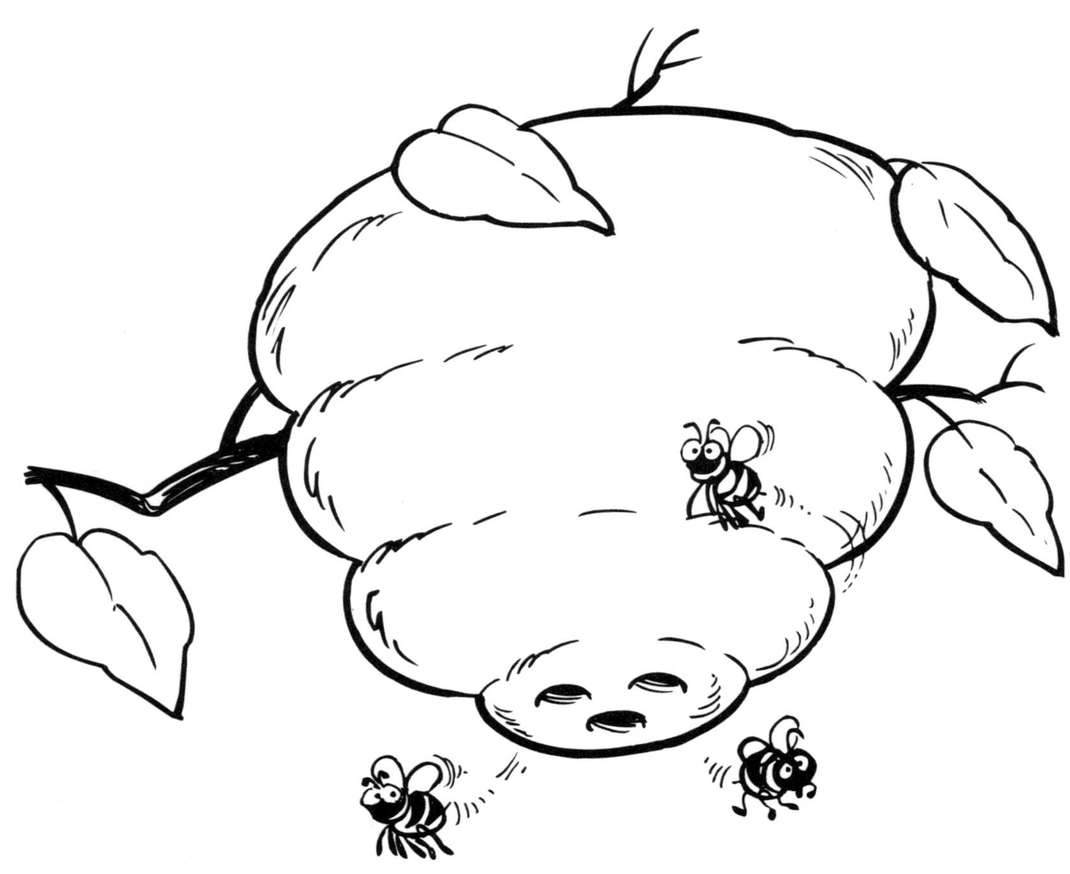

Bees live in a hive.

Some bees make honey.

Concept: Bee

Yes-No Questions

1. Is a bee an animal?

2. Does a bee have four legs?

3. Does a bee have wings?

4. Does a bee have red and green stripes?

5. Does a bee say, "Bzzz"?

6. Can a bee swim?

7. Can a bee sting?

8. Does a bee live in a house?

9. Do some bees make honey?

10. Is a bee big?

Wh- and How Questions

1. How many legs does a bee have?

2. What colors are a bee's stripes?

3. What sound does a bee make?

4. How can a bee hurt people?

5. How do bees move?

6. Where do bees live?

7. What do bees make?

8. What is a bee: a food or an animal?

9. Why do bees have wings?

10. What lives in a hive?

Bee Generalization Page

Circle the bees. Put an X on each picture that is not a bee.

Bee Mini-Book

Copy this page. Cut apart the boxes on the dotted lines. Put the story in order to make a little book and staple.

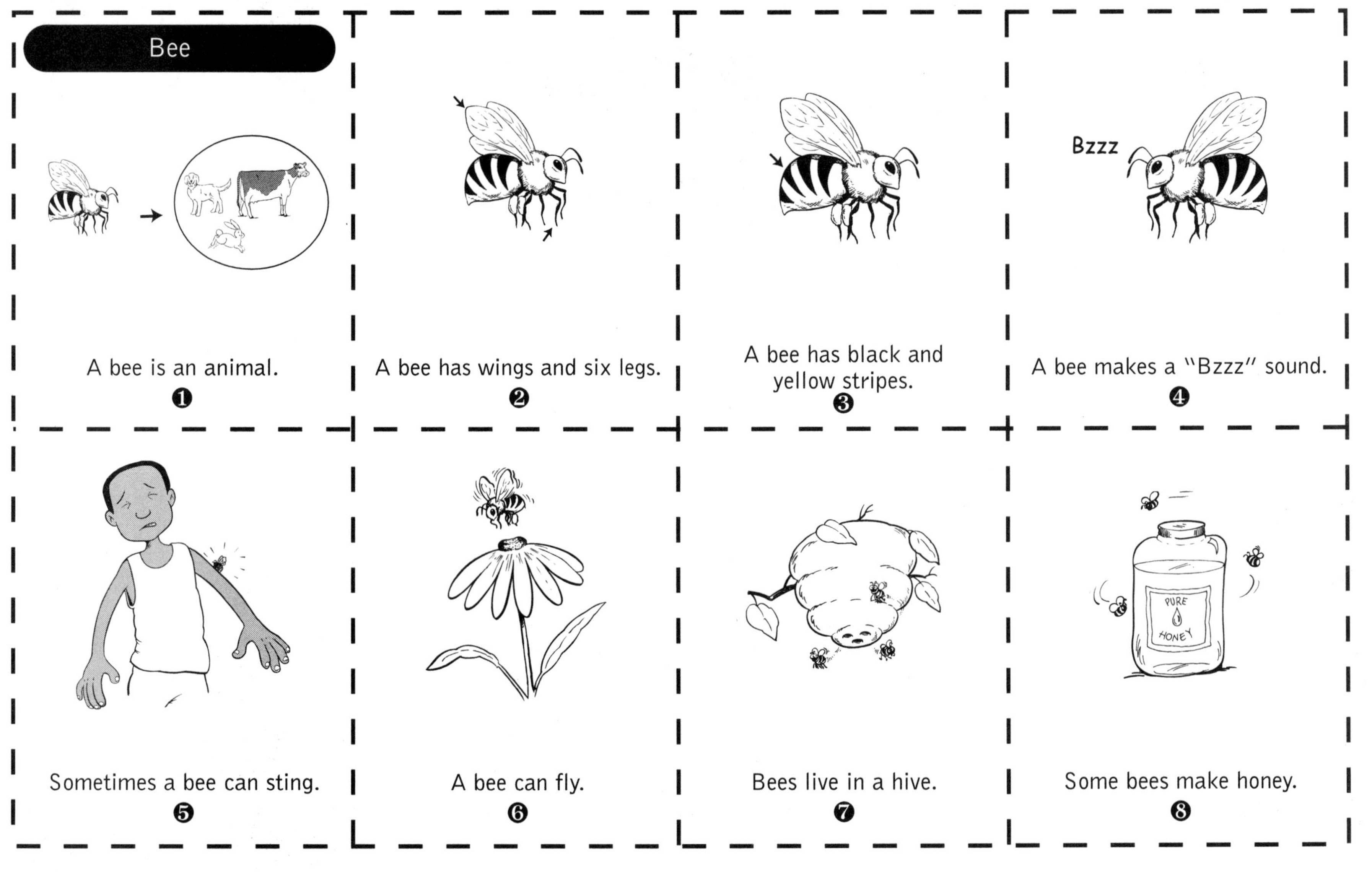

Bee
Autism & PDD: Concept Development

Snake

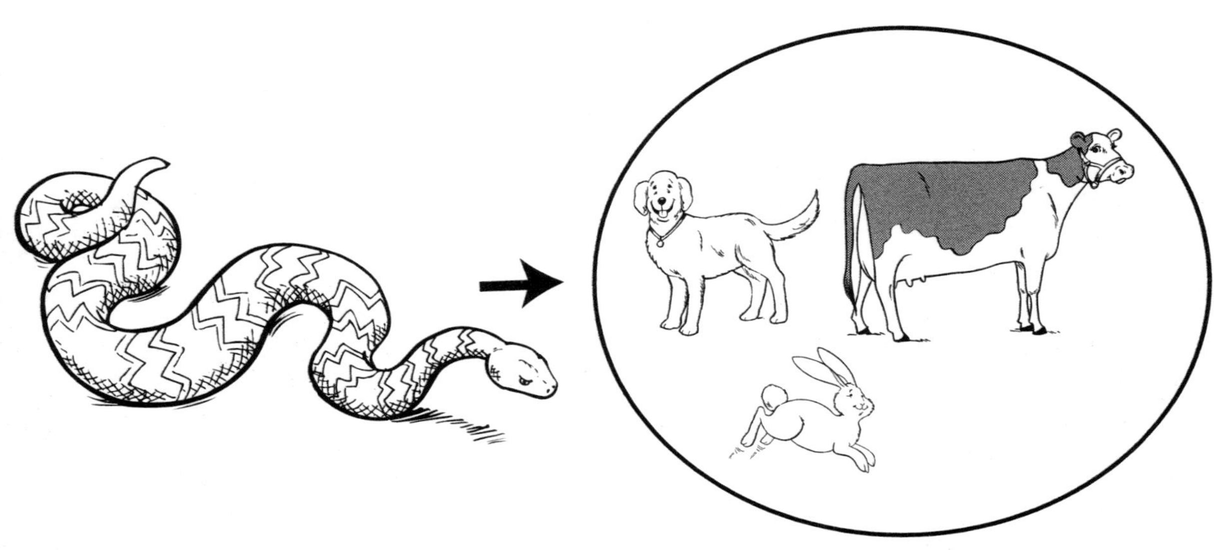

A snake is an animal.

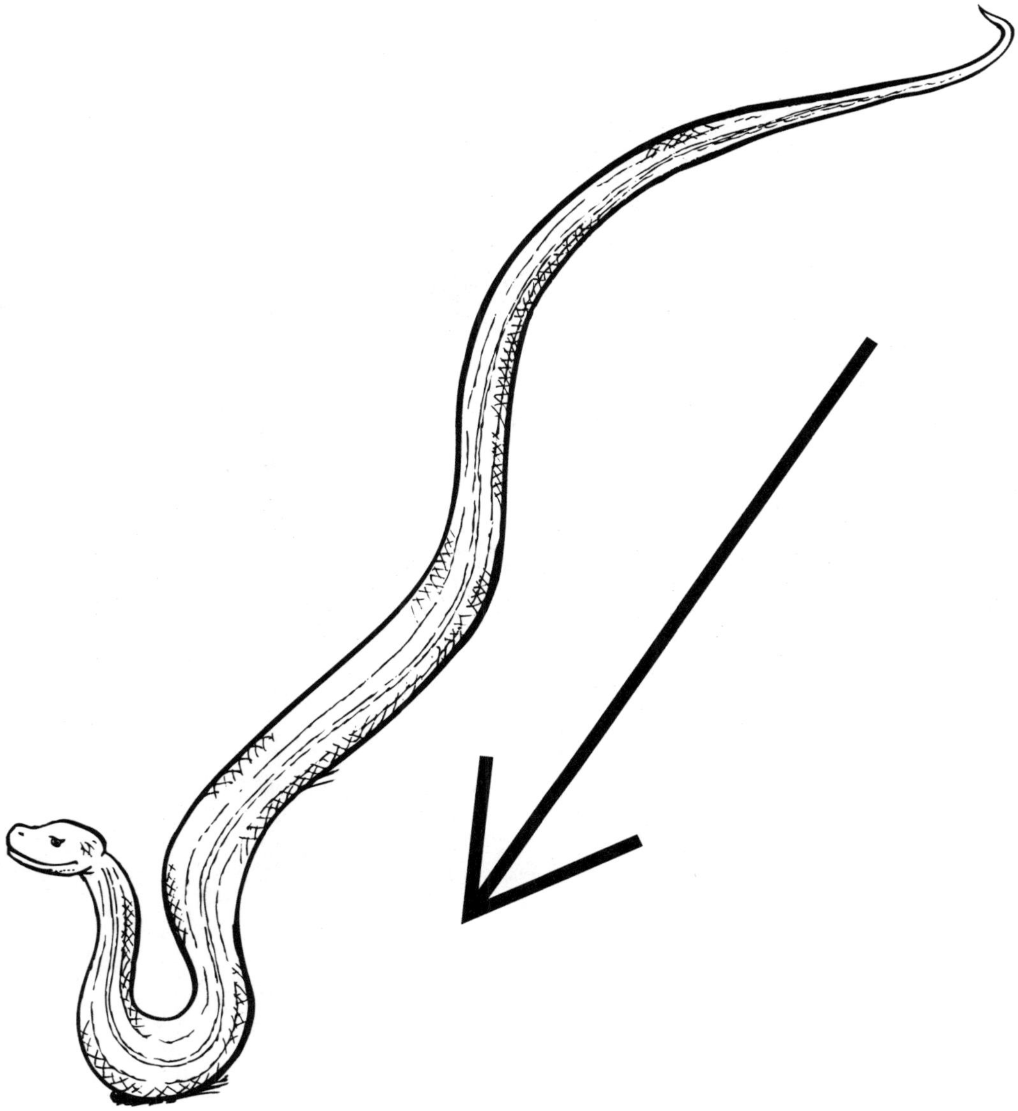

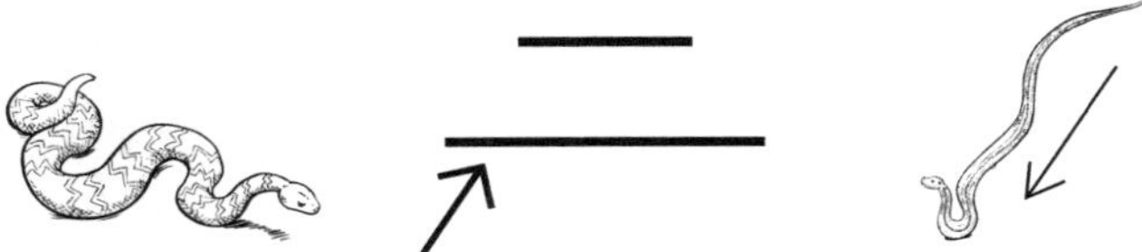

A snake has a long body.

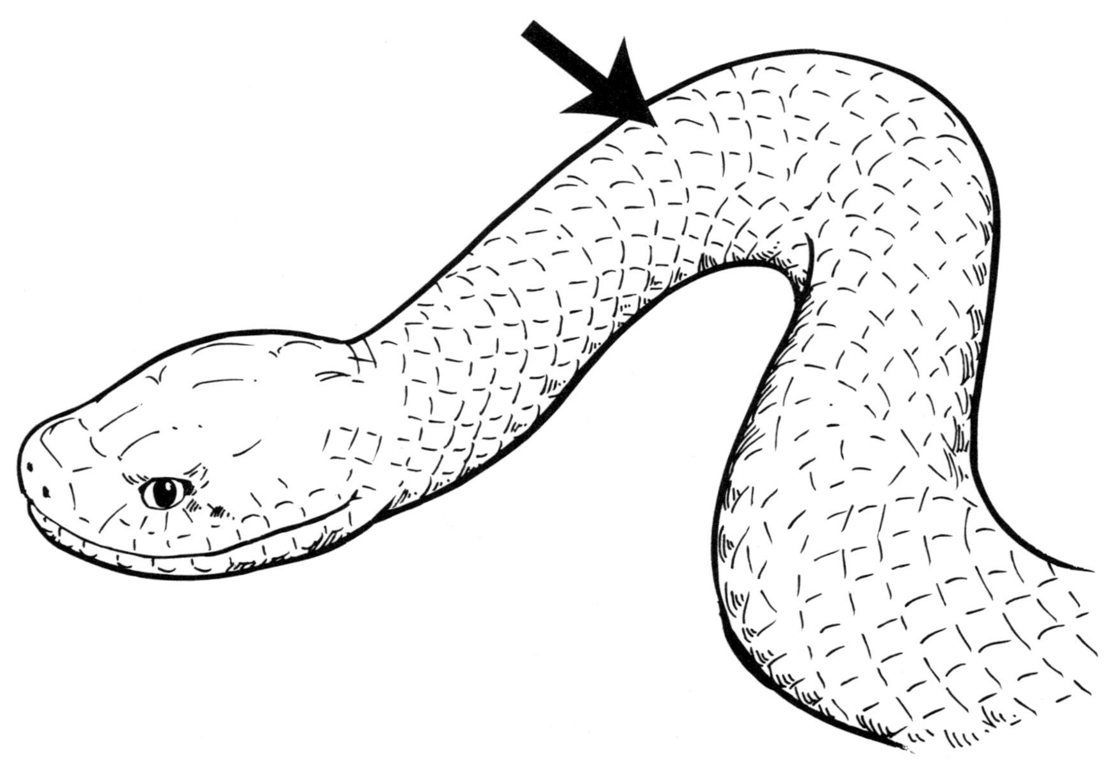

A snake has scales.

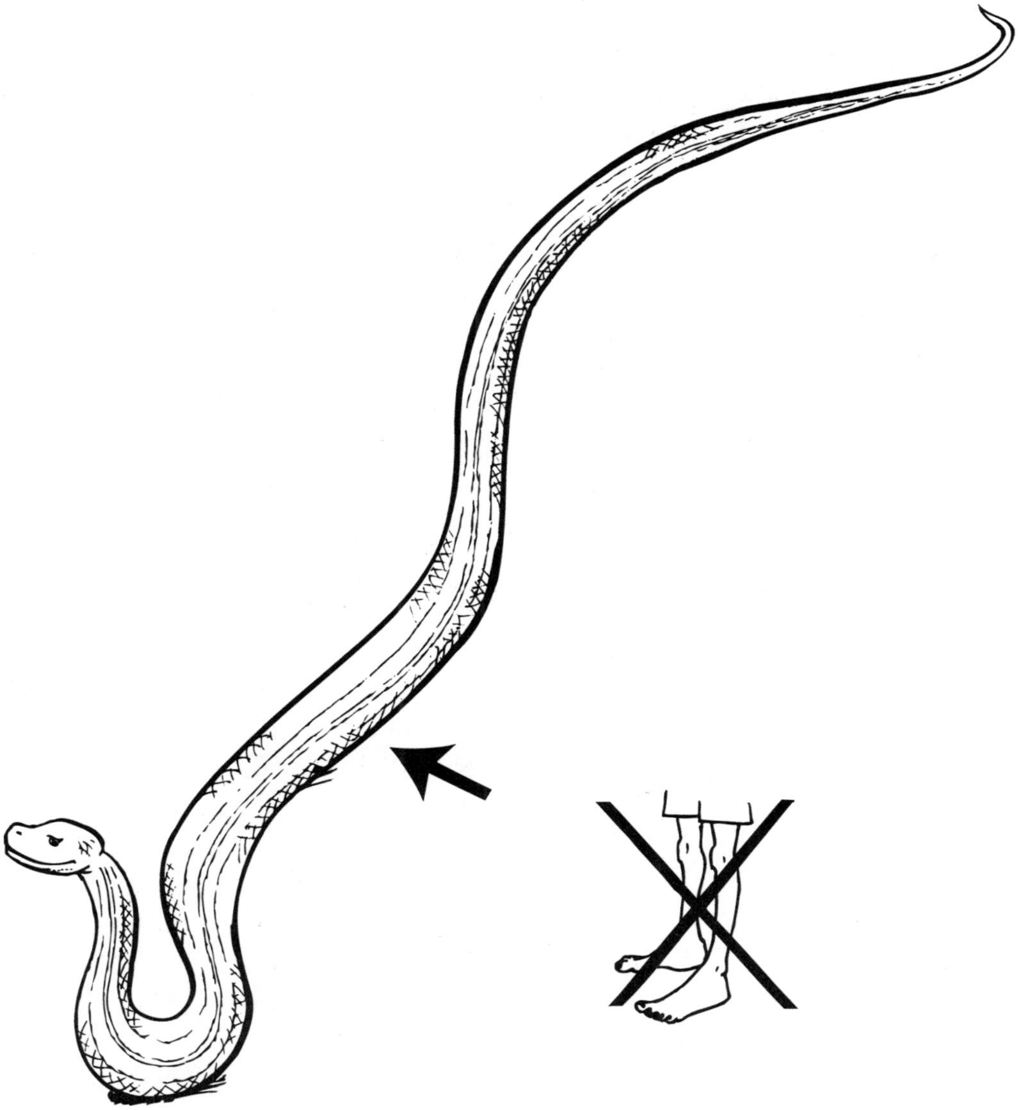

A snake has no legs.

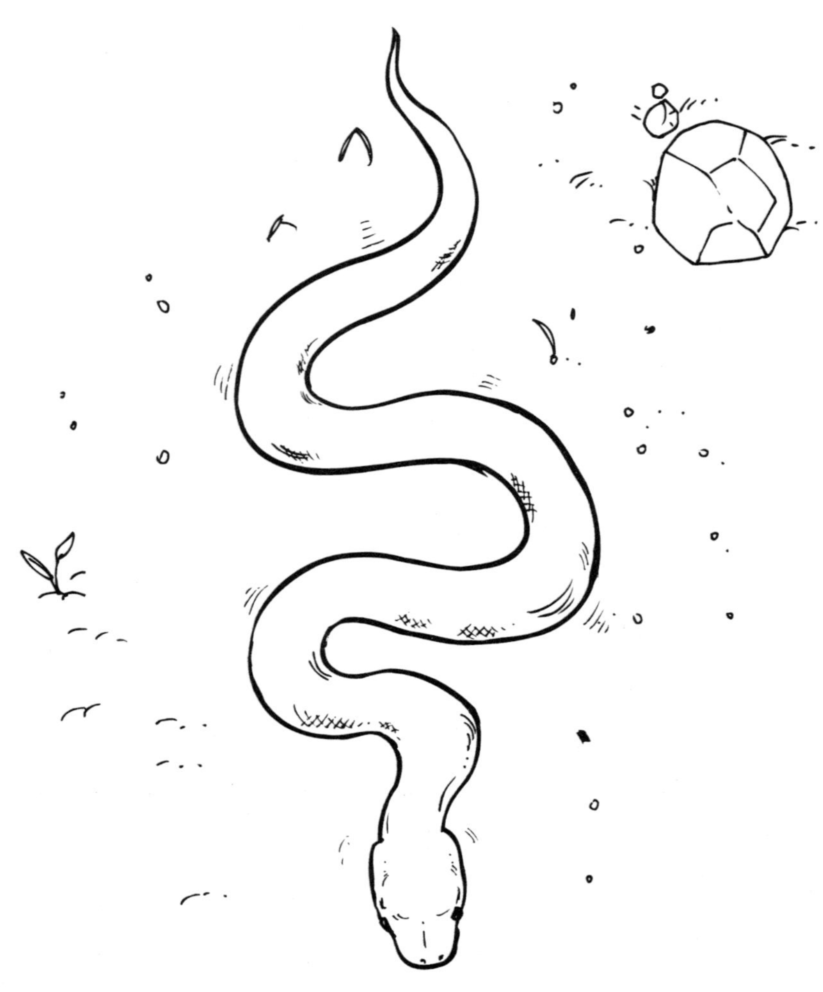

Some snakes slither on the ground.

Some snakes swim in the water.

Some snakes are big. Some snakes are little.

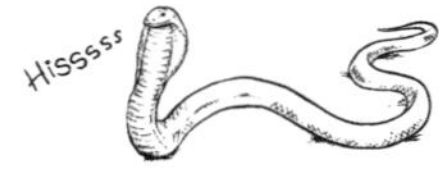

Snakes make a "Hissss" sound.

Concept: Snake

Yes-No Questions

1. Is a snake an animal?
2. Does a snake have a short body?
3. Does a snake have scales?
4. Does a snake have legs?
5. Do snakes walk on the ground?
6. Are all snakes the same size?
7. Can some snakes swim?
8. Do snakes make a "Hissss" sound?
9. Do snakes slither on the ground?
10. Do snakes have fur?

Wh- and How Questions

1. How many legs does a snake have?
2. What is a snake: a toy or an animal?
3. What covers a snake's body?
4. How do snakes move on the ground?
5. Where do some snakes swim?
6. What sound does a snake make?
7. What sizes can snakes be?
8. Where do snakes slither?
9. How do snakes move in the water?
10. What other animal has scales?

Snake Generalization Page

Circle the snakes. Put an X on each picture that is not a snake.

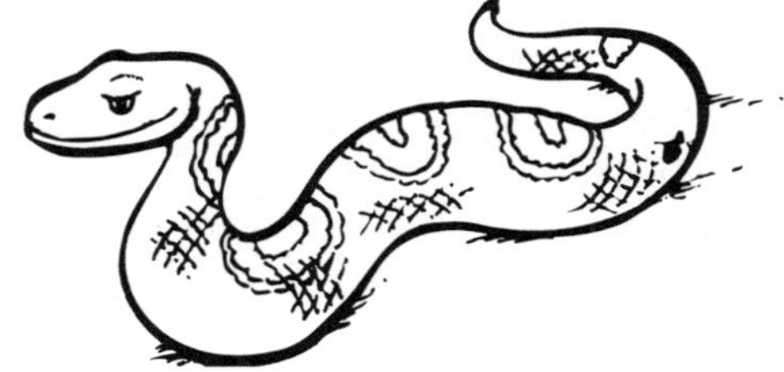

Snake Mini-Book

Copy this page. Cut apart the boxes on the dotted lines. Put the story in order to make a little book and staple.

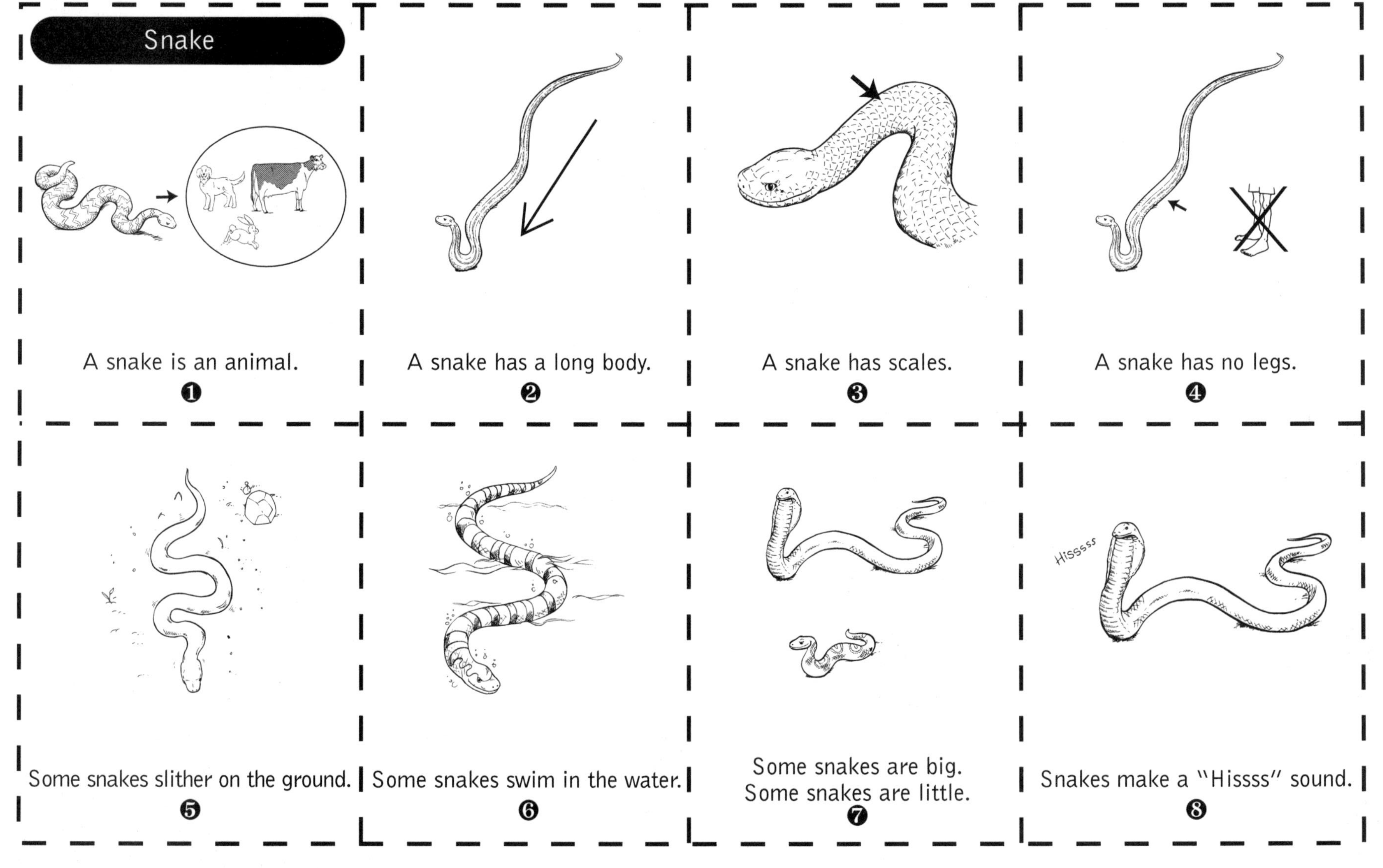

A snake is an animal.
❶

A snake has a long body.
❷

A snake has scales.
❸

A snake has no legs.
❹

Some snakes slither on the ground.
❺

Some snakes swim in the water.
❻

Some snakes are big.
Some snakes are little.
❼

Snakes make a "Hissss" sound.
❽

Snake
Autism & PDD: Concept Development

Horse

A horse is an animal.

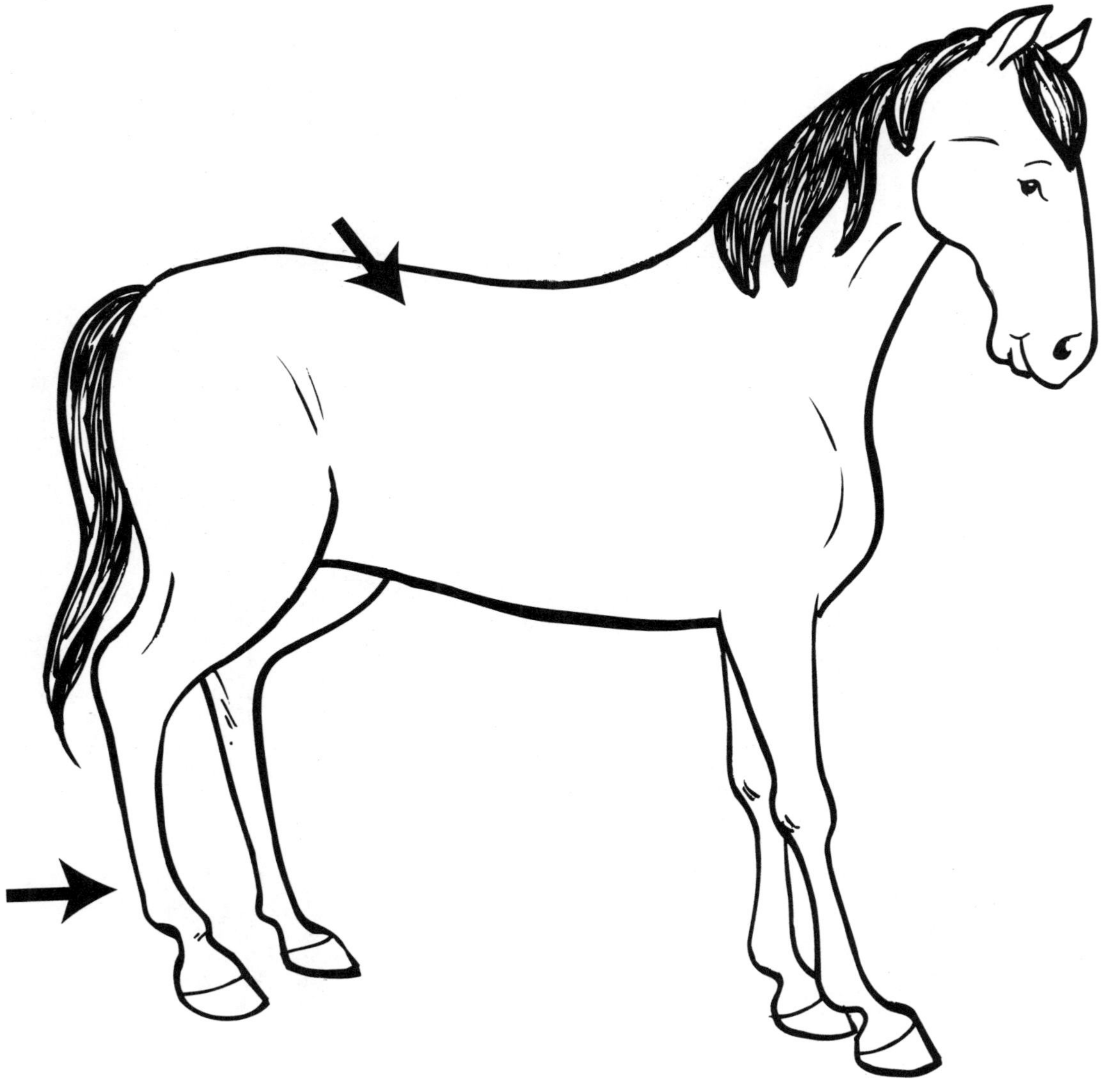

 4

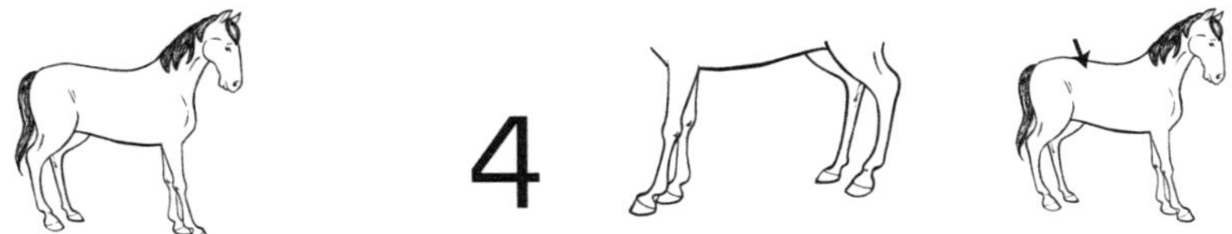

A horse has four legs and fur.

  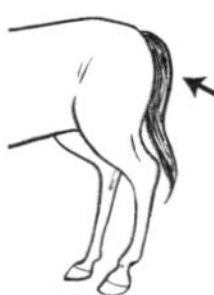

A horse has a mane and a tail.

Neigh

A horse says, "Neigh."

A horse lives on a farm.

A horse eats grass and hay.

foal

A baby horse is called a foal.

People ride horses.

Concept: Horse

Yes-No Questions

1. Is a horse a toy?

2. Does a horse have four legs?

3. Does a horse have feathers?

4. Does a horse say, "Neigh"?

5. Does a horse live in a hive?

6. Does a horse eat grass and hay?

7. Is a baby horse called a kitten?

8. Do people ride horses?

9. Is a horse an animal?

10. Does a horse have wings?

Wh- and How Questions

1. What is a horse: a toy or an animal?

2. How many legs does a horse have?

3. What covers a horse's body?

4. Where is the horse's mane?

5. What does a horse say?

6. Where does a horse live?

7. What does a horse eat?

8. What is a baby horse called?

9. Who rides horses?

10. What other animals live on a farm?

Horse Generalization Page

Circle the horses. Put an X on each picture that is not a horse.

Horse Mini-Book

Copy this page. Cut apart the boxes on the dotted lines. Put the story in order to make a little book and staple.

Horse
Autism & PDD: Concept Development

Cow

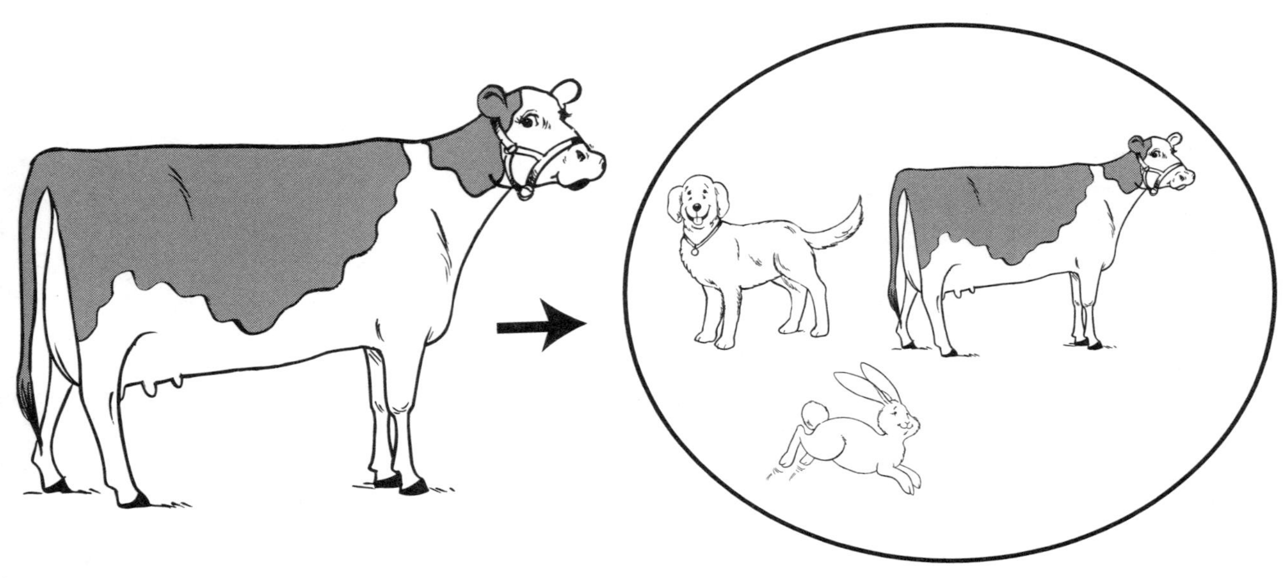

A cow is an animal.

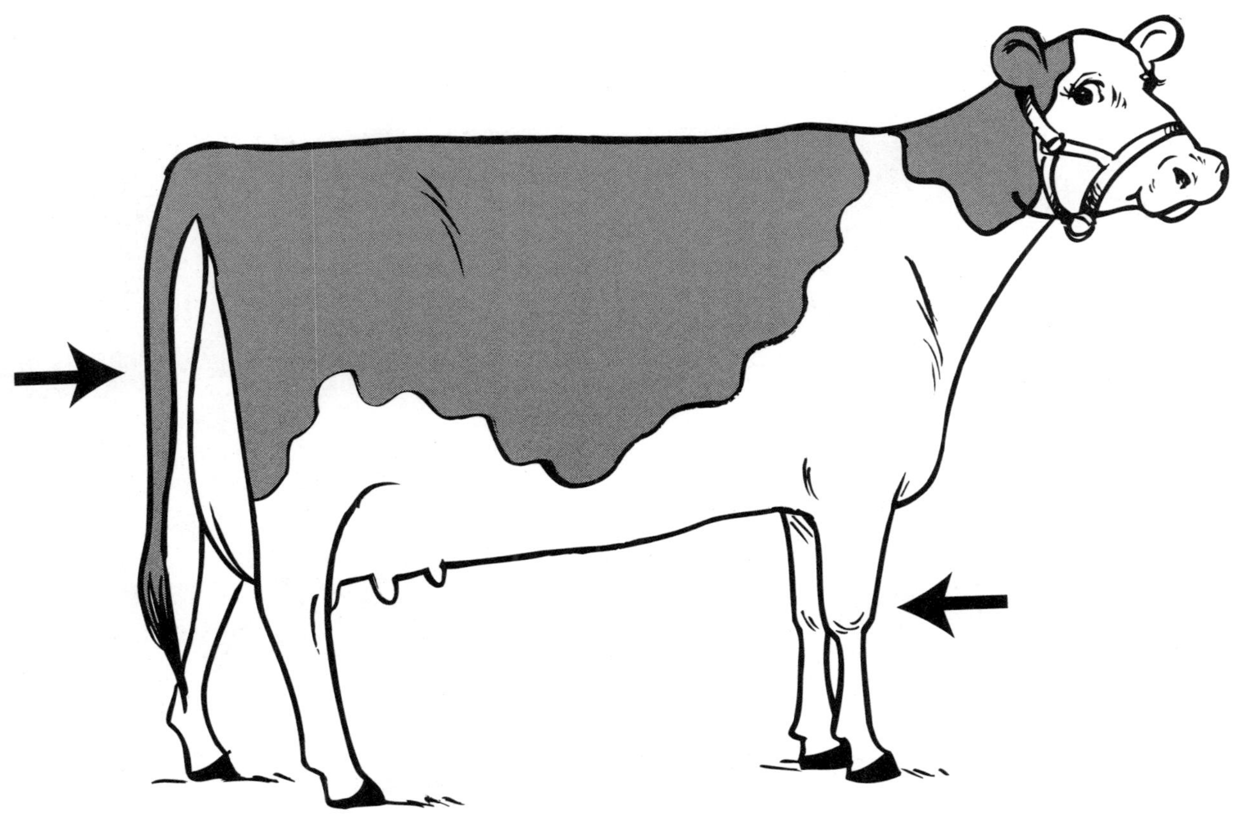

 4  

A cow has four legs and a tail.

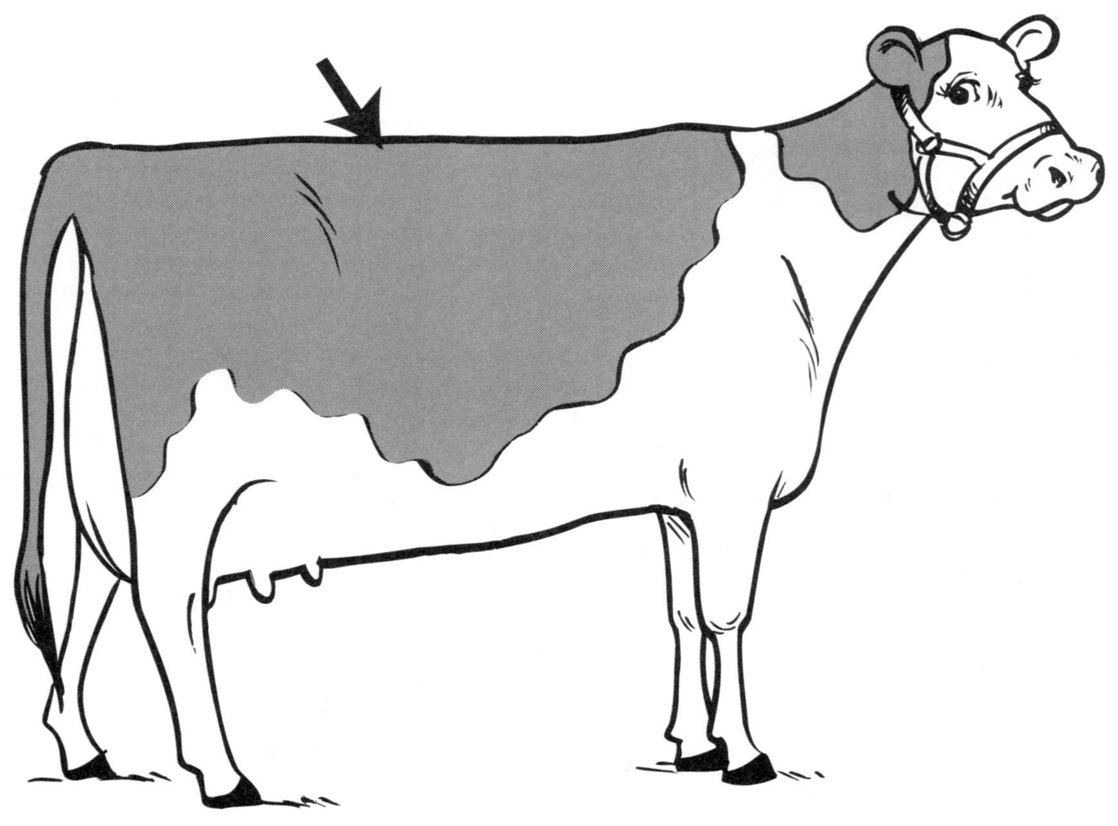

A cow has fur.

A cow says, "Mooo."

A cow eats grass and hay.

A cow lives on a farm.

A baby cow is called a calf.

Cows make milk.

Concept: Cow

Yes-No Questions

1. Is a cow an animal?
2. Does a cow have fur?
3. Does a cow bark?
4. Does a cow eat bananas?
5. Does a cow live on a farm?
6. Is a baby cow called a puppy?
7. Is a baby cow called a calf?
8. Does a cow make honey?
9. Does a cow make milk?
10. Does a cow have wings?

Wh- and How Questions

1. What is a cow: furniture or an animal?
2. How many legs does a cow have?
3. What covers a cow's body?
4. What does a cow say?
5. What does a cow eat?
6. Where does a cow live?
7. What is a baby cow called?
8. What do cows make?
9. What other animal has four legs and a tail?
10. What do you like to drink?

Cow Generalization Page

Circle the cows. Put an X on each picture that is not a cow.

Cow Mini-Book

Copy this page. Cut apart the boxes on the dotted lines. Put the story in order to make a little book and staple.

Cow
Autism & PDD: Concept Development

Chicken

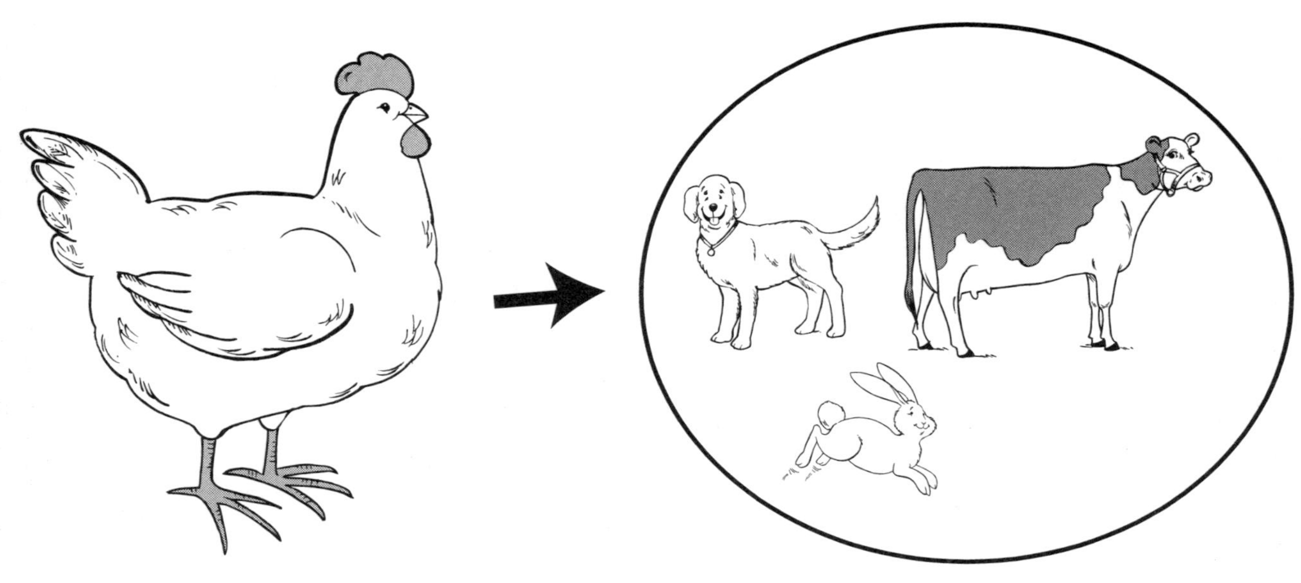

A chicken is an animal.

 2  

A chicken has two legs and a beak.

A chicken has feathers.

Cluck, Cluck

A chicken says, "Cluck, Cluck."

Chickens live on a farm.

A baby chicken is called a chick.

 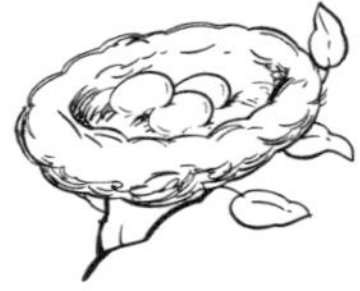

A chicken lays eggs.

  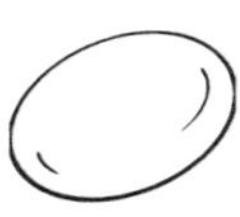

People eat chicken and their eggs.

Concept: Chicken

Yes-No Questions

1. Is a chicken an animal?
2. Does a chicken have four legs?
3. Does a chicken have a beak?
4. Does a chicken have fur?
5. Does a chicken say, "Cluck, cluck"?
6. Does a chicken live in water?
7. Is a baby chicken called a foal?
8. Do chickens lay eggs?
9. Do people eat chickens?
10. Do you like to eat chicken?

Wh- and How Questions

1. How many legs does a chicken have?
2. What is a chicken's mouth called?
3. What covers a chicken's body?
4. What other animal has feathers?
5. What does a chicken say?
6. Where does a chicken live?
7. What is a baby chicken called?
8. What does a chicken lay?
9. What other animal lays eggs?
10. Who eats chicken?

Chicken Generalization Page

Circle the chickens. Put an X on each picture that is not a chicken.

Chicken Mini-Book

Copy this page. Cut apart the boxes on the dotted lines. Put the story in order to make a little book and staple.

Autism & PDD: Concept Development

Extension Activity

Copy the scene on this page and page 130. Cut them out and tape them together to make one big scene. Place the animals from page 131 on the scene as you talk about them.

Autism & PDD: Concept Development

Extension Activity, *continued*

Copy the scene on this page and page 129. Cut them out and tape them together to make one big scene. Place the animals from page 131 on the scene as you talk about them.

Cut out these animals. Use them with the scene on pages 129 and 130.

Suggested Literature

Animals

What's Black and White and Moos?
   by Rebel Williams
Can You See It? by Cori M. Murray
Farm Noises by Jane Miller
Farm Animals Photographs by Philip Dowell
Animals Grow by Colin Walker
Open the Barn Door by Christopher Santoro

Dog

My Dog Got Away! by Cass Hollander
Dogs by Pauline Cartwright
Puppies by Jan Pfloog

Cat

Kittens A Golden Book
Great Pal Kitten by Michael Twinn
Cats: A First Discovery Book
   by Gallimard Jeunesse & Pascal de Bourgoing
Cats by Graham Meadows

Bird

The Migration by Sandra Iversen
I Can Fly by Joy Cowley
Feathers for Lunch by Lois Ehlert

Fish

Fish by Colin Walker
Animal Families by Covent Garden Books

Rabbit

Animal Fun with Bunny
   by Joshua Morris Publishing, Inc.
Animal Playtime: Bunnies
   by Cathy Drinkwater Better

Bee

Bumble Bee by Margaret Wise Brown
Honey Bee's Busy Day by Richard Fowler
Bees and Honey by Steve Pattrick

Snake

Snakes by Rebel Williams
Snakes by Claudette C. Mitchell,
   Grace R. Porter, & Patricia Cousin

Horse

Horses & Ponies illustrated by Miranda Grey

Cow

Brown Cow, Green Grass, Yellow Mellow Sun
   by Ellen B. Jackson

Chicken

From Egg to Chicken by Gerald Legg
I Bought a Baby Chicken by Kelly Milner Halls

1-03-9876543